The Prayer of Jabez

The BreakThrough Series

LITTLE BOOKS   BIG CHANGE

The
PRAYER

Breaking Through to the Blessed Life

of JABEZ

DR. BRUCE H.
WILKINSON

BOOKSPAN LARGE PRINT EDITION

Multnomah Publishers® *Sisters, Oregon*

This Large Print Edition, prepared especially for Bookspan, Inc., contains the complete, unabridged text of the original Publisher's Edition.

The Prayer of Jabez published by Multnomah Publishers, Inc.

© 2000 by Bruce H. Wilkinson

ISBN: 0-7394-2472-6

Cover image by Tatsuhiko Shimada/Photonika

Cover design by David Carlson Design

Scripture quotations are from:
The Holy Bible, New King James Version (NKJV)
© 1984 by Thomas Nelson, Inc.

Also quoted: *The Living Bible* (TLB) © 1971. Used by permission of Tyndale House Publishers, Inc. All rights reserved.

Multnomah is a trademark of Multnomah Publishers, Inc. and is registered in the U.S. Patent and Trademark Office. The colophon is a trademark of Multnomah Publishers, Inc.

Printed in the United States of America

For information:
MULTNOMAH PUBLISHERS, INC.
POST OFFICE BOX 1720
SISTERS, OREGON 97759

**This Large Print Book carries the
Seal of Approval of N.A.V.H.**

TABLE OF CONTENTS

To all who—like those Christians in the book of Acts—look at who they are now and who they'll never be, and what they can do now and what they'll never be able to do . . . and still ask God for the world.

Without the friendship, commitment, and skill of editors David Kopp and Larry Libby and the encouragement of publisher John Van Diest, the message of this book would not have found its way to paper. I am so thankful that the Lord brought us together.

PREFACE

Dear Reader,

I want to teach you how to pray a daring prayer that God always answers. It is brief—only one sentence with four parts—and tucked away in the Bible, but I believe it contains the key to a life of extraordinary favor with God.

This petition has radically changed what I experience every day by His power. In fact, thousands of believers who are applying its truths are seeing miracles happen on a regular basis.

Will you join me for a personal exploration of Jabez?

I hope you will!

Bruce H. Wilkinson

1

Little Prayer, Giant Prize

Jabez called on the God of Israel.

The little book you're holding is about what happens when ordinary Christians decide to reach for an extraordinary life—which, as it turns out, is exactly the kind God promises.

My own story starts in a kitchen with yellow counters and Texas-sized raindrops pelting the window. It was my senior year of seminary in Dallas. Darlene, my wife, and I were finding ourselves spending more and more time thinking and praying about what would come next. Where should I throw my energy, passion, and training? What did God want for us as a couple? I stood in our kitchen thinking again about a challenge I'd heard from the seminary chaplain, Dr. Richard Seume. "Want a bigger vision for your life?" he had asked earlier that week. "Sign up to be a gimper for God."

A gimper, as Seume explained it, was someone who always does a little more than what's required or expected. In the furniture business, for example, gimping is putting the finishing touches on the upholstery, patiently applying the ornamental extras that are a mark of quality and value.

Dr. Seume took as his text the briefest of Bible biographies: "Now Jabez was more honorable than his brothers" (1 Chronicles 4:9). Jabez wanted to be more and do more for God, and—as we discover by the end of verse 10—God granted him his request.

End of verse. End of Bible story.

What sentence has revolutionized my life the most? The cry of a gimper named Jabez.

Lord, I think I want to be a gimper for you, I prayed as I looked out the window at the blustery spring rain. But I was puzzled. *What exactly did Jabez do to rise above the rest? Why did God answer his prayer?* I wondered. For that matter, why did God even include Jabez's miniprofile in the Bible?

Maybe it was the raindrops running down the windowpanes. Suddenly my thoughts ran past verse 9.

I picked up my Bible and read verse 10— the prayer of Jabez. Something in his prayer would explain the mystery. It had to. Pulling a chair up to the yellow counter, I bent over my Bible, and reading the prayer over and over, I searched with all my heart for the future God had for someone as ordinary as I.

The next morning, I prayed Jabez's prayer word for word.

And the next.

And the next.

Thirty years later, I haven't stopped.

If you were to ask me what sentence—other than my prayer for salvation—has revolutionized my life and ministry the most, I would tell you that it was the cry of a gimper named Jabez, who is still remembered not for what he did, but for what he prayed—and for what happened next.

In the pages of this little book, I want to introduce you to the amazing truths in Jabez's prayer for blessing and prepare you to expect God's astounding answers to it *as a regular part of your life experience.*

How do I know that it will significantly impact you? Because of my experience and the testimony of hundreds of others around the world with whom I've shared these principles. Because, even more importantly, the Jabez prayer distills God's powerful will for your future. Finally, because it reveals that your Father longs to give you so much more than you may have ever thought to ask for.

Just ask the man who had no future.

THE PRODIGY OF THE GENEALOGY

Someone once said there is really very little difference between people—but that little difference makes a great deal of difference.

Something about this man caused the historian to pause, clear his throat, and switch tactics.

Jabez doesn't stand astride the Old Testament like a Moses or a David or light up the book of Acts like those early Christians who turned the world upside down. But one thing is sure: The little difference in his life made all the difference.

You could think of him as the Prodigy of the Genealogy, or maybe the Bible's Little Big Man. You'll find him hiding in the least-read section of one of the least-read books of the Bible.

The first nine chapters of 1 Chronicles are taken up with the official family tree of the Hebrew tribes, beginning with Adam and proceeding through thousands of years to Israel's return from captivity. Talk about boring! The long lists of unfamiliar and difficult names—more than five hundred of them—are likely to make even the bravest Bible student turn back.

Take chapter 4. *The descendants of Judah: Perez, Hezron, and Carmi, and Hur, and Shobal. . . .* And that's just the beginning.

Ahumai
Ishma
Idbash
Hazelelponi
Anub . . .

I'd forgive you if you suddenly considered putting this little book aside and reaching for your TV remote. But stay with me. Because forty-four names into the chapter, a story suddenly breaks through:

> Now Jabez was more honorable than his brothers, and his mother called his name Jabez, saying, "Because I bore him in pain." And Jabez called on the God of Israel saying, "Oh, that You would bless me indeed, and enlarge my territory, that Your hand would be with me, and that You would keep me

from evil, that I may not cause pain!" So God granted him what he requested. (1 Chronicles 4:9–10)

In the next verse, the roll call for the tribe of Judah picks up as if nothing has happened—*Chelub, Shuah, Mehir. . . .*

Something about this man Jabez had caused the historian to pause in middrone, clear his throat, and switch tactics. "Ah, wait a minute!" he seems to interject. "You just *gotta* know something about this guy named Jabez. He stands head and shoulders above the rest!"

Just under the surface of each request lies a giant paradigm breaker.

What was the secret to the enduring reputation of Jabez? You can search from front to back in your Bible, as I have, and you won't find any more information than we have in these two brief verses:

- Things started badly for a person no one had ever heard of.
- He prayed an unusual, one-sentence prayer.
- Things ended extraordinarily well.

Clearly, the outcome can be traced to his prayer. Something about Jabez's simple, direct request to God changed his life and left a permanent mark on the history books of Israel:

Oh, that You would bless me indeed,
and enlarge my territory,
that Your hand would be with me,
and that You would keep
me from evil.

At first glance, the four requests may strike you as sincere, sensible, even noble, but not terribly remarkable. Yet just under the surface of each lies a giant paradigm breaker that runs exactly opposite to the way you and I usually think. In the pages to come, I want to show you just how dramatically each of Jabez's requests can release something miraculous in your life.

LIVING BEYOND THE LIMITS

When was the last time God worked through you in such a way that you knew beyond doubt that God had done it? In fact, when was the last time you saw miracles happen on a regular basis in *your* life? If you're like most believers I've met, you wouldn't know how to ask for that kind of experience, or even if you should.

What I have to share with you has been opening up lives to God's mighty working for many years. Recently, I was in Dallas to teach on the Jabez blessing to an audience of 9,000. Later over lunch, a man said to me, "Bruce, I heard you preach the message of Jabez fifteen years ago, and I haven't stopped praying it. The change has been so overwhelming I have just never stopped."

When was the last time God worked through you in such a way that you knew beyond doubt God had done it?

Across the table, another friend agreed. He said he'd been praying Jabez's little prayer for ten years with similar results. The man next to him, a heart surgeon from Indianapolis, said he had been praying it for five.

I told them, "Friends, I've been praying Jabez for more than *half my life!*"

Because you're reading this book, I believe you share my desire to reach for a life that will be "more honorable" for God. Not that you wish others to reach for less, but for you, nothing but God's fullest blessing will do. When you stand before Him to give your accounting, your deepest longing is to hear, "Well done!"

God really does have unclaimed blessings waiting for you, my friend. I know it sounds impossible—even embarrassingly suspicious in our self-serving day. Yet that very exchange—your want for God's plenty—has been His loving will for your life from eternity past. And with a handful of core commitments on your part, you can proceed from this day forward with the confidence and expectation that your heavenly Father will bring it to pass for you.

Think of it this way: Instead of standing near the river's edge, asking for a cup of water to get you through each day, you'll do something unthinkable—you will take the little prayer with the giant prize and *jump into the river!* At that moment, you will begin to let the loving currents of God's grace and power carry you along. God's great plan for you will surround you and sweep you forward into the profoundly important and satisfying life He has waiting.

If that is what you want, keep reading.

2

So Why
Not Ask?

Oh, that you would bless me indeed!

You're at a spiritual retreat in the mountains with others who want to experience a fuller Christian life. For the duration of the retreat everyone has been matched with a mentor. Yours is in his seventies, and he's been touching lives for God longer than you've been alive.

On the way to the showers the first morning, you walk past his room. His door is ajar, and he has just knelt down to pray. You can't resist. *How exactly does a giant of the faith begin his prayers?* you wonder.

You pause and lean closer. Will he pray for revival? Pray for the hungry around the world? Pray for you?

But this is what you hear: "O Lord, I beg you first and most this morning, please bless . . . *me!*"

Startled at such a selfish prayer, you pad down the hall to your shower. But as you're adjusting the water temperature, a thought hits you. It's so obvious, you can't believe you haven't thought it before:

Great men of the faith think differently than the rest of us.

By the time you're dressed and heading for breakfast, you're sure of it. The reason some men and women of faith rise above the rest, you decide, is that they think and pray differently than those around them.

Is it possible that God wants you to be "selfish" in your prayers? To ask for more—and more again—from your Lord? I've met so many earnest Christians who take it as a sign of immaturity to think such thoughts. They assume they'll seem impolite or greedy if they ask God for too many blessings.

Is it possible that God wants you to be more "selfish" in your prayers?

Maybe you think like that. If you do, I want to show you that such a prayer is not the self-centered act it might appear, but a supremely spiritual one and exactly the kind of request our Father longs to hear.

First, let's take a closer look at Jabez's story.

NOT PAIN, BUT GAIN

As far as we can tell, Jabez lived in southern Israel after the conquest of Canaan and during the time of the judges. He was born into the tribe of Judah and eventually became the notable head of a clan. Yet his story really begins with his name: "His mother called his name Jabez, saying, 'Because I bore him in pain.'"

In Hebrew, the word *Jabez* means "pain." A literal rendering could read, "He causes (or will cause) pain."

He grew up with a name any boy would love to hate.

Doesn't sound like the start of a promising life, does it?

All babies arrive with a certain amount of pain, but something about Jabez's birth went beyond the usual—so much so that his mother chose to memorialize it in her son's name. Why? The pregnancy or the delivery may have been traumatic. Perhaps the baby was born breech. Or perhaps the mother's pain was emotional—maybe the child's father abandoned her during the pregnancy; maybe he had died; maybe the family had fallen into such financial straits that the prospect of another mouth to feed brought only fear and worry.

Only God knows for sure what caused the pain of this anguished mother. Not that it made much difference to young Jabez. He grew up with a name any boy would love to hate. Imagine if you had to go through childhood enduring the teasing of bullies, the daily reminders of your unwelcome arrival, and mocking questions like, "So, young man, what *was* your mother thinking?"

Yet by far the heaviest burden of Jabez's name was how it defined his future. In Bible times, a man and his name were so intimately related that "to cut off the name" of an individual amounted to the same thing as killing him. A name was often taken as a wish for or prophecy about the child's future. For example, Jacob can mean "grabber," a good one-word biography for that scheming patriarch. Naomi and her husband named their two sons Mahlon and Chilion. Translation? "Puny" and "pining." And that was exactly what they were. Both of them died in early adulthood. Solomon means "peace," and sure enough, he became the first king of Israel to reign without going to war. A name that meant "pain" didn't bode well for Jabez's future.

Despite his dismal prospects, Jabez found a way out. He had grown up hearing about the God of Israel who had freed his forefathers from slavery, rescued them from powerful enemies, and established them in a land of plenty. By the time he was an adult, Jabez believed and fervently hoped in this God of miracles and new beginnings.

When we ask God's blessing, we're not asking for more of what we could get for ourselves.

So why not ask for one?

That's what he did. He prayed the biggest, most improbable request imaginable:

"Oh, that You would bless me *indeed* . . . !"

I love the urgency, the personal vulnerability of his plea. In Hebrew, adding "indeed" to this prayer was like adding five exclamation points, or writing the request in capital letters and underlining it.

In my mind's eye, I picture Jabez standing

before a massive gate recessed into a sky-high wall. Weighed down by the sorrow of his past and the dreariness of his present, he sees before him only impossibility—a future shut off. But raising his hands to heaven, he cries out, "Father, oh, Father! Please bless me! And what I really mean is . . . bless me a lot!"

With the last word, the transformation begins. He hears a tremendous crack. Then a groan. Then a rumble as the huge gate swings away from him in a wide arc. There, stretching to the horizon, are fields of blessings.

And Jabez steps forward into another life.

Blessing Is Not about Sneezing

Before we can ask for God's blessing with confidence, we need a clear understanding of what the word means. We hear "bless" or "blessing" intoned from every pulpit. We ask God to bless the missionaries, the kids, and the food we're about to eat. It's something Grandma says when she hears you sneeze.

No wonder the meaning of blessing gets watered down to something vague and innocuous like "Have a nice day." No wonder so many Christians aren't as desperate as Jabez was to receive it!

To bless in the biblical sense means to ask for or to impart supernatural favor. When we ask for God's blessing, we're not asking for more of what we could get for ourselves. We're crying out for the wonderful, unlimited goodness that only God has the power to know about or give to us. This kind of richness is what the writer was referring to in Proverbs: "The Lord's blessing is our greatest wealth; all our work adds nothing to it" (Proverbs 10:22, TLB).

Notice a radical aspect of Jabez's request for blessing: *He left it entirely up to God to decide what the blessings would be and where, when, and how Jabez would receive them.* This kind of radical trust in God's good intentions toward us has nothing in common with the popular gospel that you should ask God for a Cadillac, a six-figure income, or some other material sign that you have found a way to cash in on your connection with Him. Instead, the Jabez blessing focuses like a laser on our wanting for ourselves nothing more and nothing less than what God wants for us.

When we seek God's blessing as the ultimate value in life, we are throwing ourselves entirely into the river of His will and power and purposes for us. All our other needs become secondary to what we really want— which is to become wholly immersed in what God is trying to do in us, through us, and around us for His glory.

Let me tell you a guaranteed by-product of sincerely seeking His blessing: Your life will become marked by miracles. How do I know? Because He promises it, and I've seen it happen in my own! God's power to accomplish great things suddenly finds no obstruction in you. You're moving in His direction. You're praying for exactly what God desires. Suddenly the unhindered forces of heaven can begin to accomplish God's perfect will—through you. And you will be the first to notice!

But there's a catch.

MR. JONES GOES TO HEAVEN

What if you found out that God had it in mind to send you twenty-three specific blessings today, but you got only one? What do you suppose the reason would be?

There's a little fable about a Mr. Jones

who dies and goes to heaven. Peter is waiting at the gates to give him a tour. Amid the splendor of golden streets, beautiful mansions, and choirs of angels that Peter shows him, Mr. Jones notices an odd-looking building. He thinks it looks like an enormous warehouse—it has no windows and only one door. But when he asks to see inside, Peter hesitates. "You really don't want to see what's in there," he tells the new arrival.

Why would there be any secrets in heaven? Jones wonders. *What incredible surprise could be waiting for me in there?* When the official tour is over he's still wondering, so he asks again to see inside the structure.

"These boxes all have names on them," Mr. Jones *muses. Turning to Peter he asks, "Do I have one?"*

Finally Peter relents. When the apostle opens the door, Mr. Jones almost knocks him over in his haste to enter. It turns out that the enormous building is filled with row after row of shelves, floor to ceiling, each stacked neatly with white boxes tied in red ribbons.

"These boxes all have names on them,"

Mr. Jones muses aloud. Then turning to Peter he asks, "Do I have one?"

"Yes, you do." Peter tries to guide Mr. Jones back outside. "Frankly," Peter says, "if I were you . . ." But Mr. Jones is already dashing toward the "J" aisle to find his box.

Peter follows, shaking his head. He catches up with Mr. Jones just as he is slipping the red ribbon off his box and popping the lid. Looking inside, Jones has a moment of instant recognition, and he lets out a deep sigh like the ones Peter has heard so many times before.

Because there in Mr. Jones's white box are all the blessings that God wanted to give to him while he was on earth . . . but Mr. Jones had never asked.

"Ask," promised Jesus, "and it will be given to you" (Matthew 7:7). "You do not have because you do not ask," said James (James 4:2). Even though there is no limit to God's goodness, if you didn't ask Him for a blessing yesterday, you didn't get all that you were supposed to have.

That's the catch—if you don't ask for His blessing, you forfeit those that come to you only when you ask. In the same way that a father is honored to have a child beg for his blessing, your Father is delighted to respond generously when His blessing is what you covet most.

GOD'S NATURE IS TO BLESS

Perhaps you think that your name is just another word for pain or trouble, or that the legacy you have been handed from your family circumstances is nothing but a liability. You just don't feel like a candidate for blessing.

Or perhaps you're one of those Christians who thinks that once you're saved, God's blessings sort of drizzle over your life at a predetermined rate, no matter what you do. No extra effort required.

Or perhaps you have slipped into a ledger-keeping mindset with God. In your blessings account you have a column for deposits and one for withdrawals. Has God been unusually kind to you lately? Then you think that you shouldn't expect, much less ask for, Him to credit your account. You might even think He should ignore you for a while, or even

I'm asking you to change the way you think.

debit your account by sending some trouble your way.

This kind of thinking is a sin and a trap! When Moses said to God on Mount Sinai, "Show me Your glory" (Exodus 33:18), he was asking for a more intimate understanding of God. In response, God described Himself as "the Lord, the Lord God, merciful and gracious, longsuffering, and abounding in goodness and truth" (34:6).

Incredible! The very nature of God is to have goodness in so much abundance that it overflows into our unworthy lives. If you think about God in any other way than that, I'm asking you to change the way you think. Why not make it a lifelong commitment to ask God every day to bless you—and while He's at it, bless you *a lot?*

God's bounty is limited only by us, not by His resources, power, or willingness to give. Jabez was blessed simply because he refused to let any obstacle, person, or opinion loom larger than God's nature. And God's nature is to bless.

His kindness in recording Jabez's story in the Bible is proof that it's not who you are, or what your parents decided for you, or what you were "fated" to be that counts. What counts is knowing who you want to be and asking for it.

Through a simple, believing prayer, you can change your future. You can change what happens one minute from now.

3

LIVING LARGE FOR GOD

*Oh, that You would enlarge
my territory!*

The next part of the Jabez prayer—a plea for more territory—is where you ask God to enlarge your life so you can make a greater impact for Him.

From both the context and the results of Jabez's prayer, we can see that there was more to his request than a simple desire for more real estate. He wanted more influence, more responsibility, and more opportunity *to make a mark for the God of Israel.*

Depending on the version you're reading, the word *territory* can also be translated *coast* or *borders.* For Jabez and his contemporaries, that word carried the same emotional power as the words *homestead* or *frontier* did for generations of American pioneers. It spoke of a place of one's own with plenty of room to grow.

In Jabez's time part of Israel's recent national history was Joshua's conquest of Canaan and the partitioning of the Promised Land into chunks of real estate for each tribe. When Jabez cried out to God, "Enlarge my territory!" he was looking at his present circumstances and concluding, "Surely I was born for more than this!" As a farmer or herdsman, he looked over the spread his family had passed down to him, ran his eye down the fence lines, visited the boundary markers, calculated the potential—and made a decision: *Everything you've put under my care, O Lord—take it, and enlarge it.*

He looked at his circumstances and concluded, "Surely I was born for more than this!"

If Jabez had worked on Wall Street, he might have prayed, "Lord, increase the value of my investment portfolios." When I talk to presidents of companies, I often talk to them about this particular mind-set. When Christian executives ask me, "Is it right for me to ask God for more business?" my response is, "Absolutely!" If you're doing your business God's way, it's not only right to ask for more, but He is waiting for you to ask. Your business is the territory God has entrusted to you. He wants you to accept it as a significant opportunity to touch individual lives, the business community, and the larger world for His glory. Asking Him to enlarge that opportunity brings Him only delight.

Suppose Jabez had been a wife and a mother. Then the prayer might have gone: "Lord, add to my family, favor my key relationships, multiply for Your glory the influence of my household." Your home is the single most powerful arena on earth to change a life for God. Why wouldn't He want you to be mighty for Him?

No matter what your vocation, the highest form of Jabez's prayer for more territory might sound something like:

O God and King, please expand my opportunities and my impact in such a way that I touch more lives for Your glory. Let me do more for You!

When you pray like this, things get pretty exciting.

MOVING THE BOUNDARY LINES

During a weeklong speaking engagement some years ago at a large Christian college

in California, I challenged students to pray
the Jabez prayer for more blessing and
greater influence. I suggested that the 2000-
member student body set a ministry goal
worthy of a college of its stature.

"Why not look at the globe and pick an island," I suggested. "When you have it
picked out, put together a team of students,
charter an airliner, then take over the island
for God."

Some students roared. Some questioned
my sanity. But nearly everyone listened. I
persisted. I had been to the island of
Trinidad and seen the
need, I told them. "You
should ask God for
Trinidad," I said. "And a
DC-10."

*"You should
ask God for
Trinidad," I said.
"And a DC-10."*

I had no immediate
takers.

Still, the challenge prompted a flurry of
stimulating conversations. I found most students eager to do something meaningful
with their time and talents, but unsure where
to start. They usually made a point of listing
their deficiencies in skill, money, courage, or
opportunity.

I spent much of that week asking a question: If the God of heaven loves you infinitely and wants you in His presence every moment, and if He knows that heaven is a much better place for you, then why on earth has He left you here? With student after student, I pressed home what I understand to be a biblical answer to that question: because God wants you to be moving out your boundary lines, taking in new territory for Him—maybe an island—and reaching people in His name.

God was at work. A week after I had returned home, I received a letter from a student named Warren. He told me that he and his friend Dave had decided to challenge God's power and ask Him to bless them and enlarge their borders. Specifically, they had prayed that God would give them the opportunity to witness to the governor of the state *that weekend.* Throwing their sleeping bags in Warren's '63 Plymouth Valiant, they had driven the 400 miles to the capital to pound on doors.

The letter continued:

By Sunday night when we got back from Sacramento, this is what had happened:

We had expressed our faith to two gas station attendants, four security guards, the head of the U.S. National Guard, the director of the Department of Health, Education, and Welfare for the state of California, the head of the California Highway Patrol, the governor's secretary, and finally the governor himself.

As God is making us grow, we are thankful and scared stiff. Thanks again for your challenge!

That was just the beginning. Over the next weeks and months, a vision for more territory swept the campus. By fall, a student team headed by Warren and Dave had mounted a major mission project for the following summer. They called it Operation Jabez. Their objective: assemble a team of self-supported student workers, charter a jet, and—you guessed it—fly to the island of Trinidad for a summer of ministry.

And that is exactly what they did. One hundred and twenty-six students and faculty signed up. By the time the jet took off fully loaded from Los Angeles, Operation Jabez boasted trained teams ready to minister through drama, construction, vacation Bible school, music, and home visitation. The college president called Operation Jabez the single most significant student ministry venture in the college's history.

Two students had asked God to enlarge their territory—and He did! One little prayer had remapped boundary lines and impacted the lives of thousands of people.

"I THINK THIS IS MY APPOINTMENT"

The Jabez prayer is a revolutionary request. Just as it is highly unusual to hear anyone pray, "God, please bless *me*!" so it is rare to hear anyone plead, "God, please give me more ministry!" Most of us think our lives are too full already. But when, in faith, you start to pray for more ministry, amazing things occur. As your opportunities expand, your ability and resources supernaturally increase, too. Right away you'll sense the pleasure God feels in your request and His urgency to accomplish great things through you.

People will show up on your doorstep or at the table next to you. They'll start saying things that surprise even them. They'll ask for something—they're not sure what—and wait for your reply.

I call these encounters Jabez appointments.

I remember the first time I asked for one. It was in a very surprising place—aboard a ship off the coast of Turkey. I was traveling alone, scouting a tour company that specialized in taking groups around the Mediterranean, following in the footsteps of the early church. We had enjoyed beautiful days aboard with plenty of

I took a table at an outdoor café and ordered a cup of coffee.

time for me to work on various projects, but I was getting lonelier by the day. The morning we anchored at Patmos, the island where John wrote the Book of Revelation, I hit bottom.

Instead of taking the guided tour, I walked around the streets of the little port talking to the Lord. *Lord, I feel so homesick and weak*, I prayed. *But I want to be your servant. Even now, enlarge my borders. Send somebody who needs me.*

Entering a small square, I took a table at an outdoor café and ordered a cup of coffee. A few minutes later I heard a man's voice behind me. "You on the cruise ship?"

I looked up to see a young man walking toward me. "Yes, I am," I said. "How about you?"

He said he was an American living on the island, then asked if he could join me. His name was Terry. Within minutes he was pouring out his story. As it turned out, his marriage was on the rocks. In fact, that day was the end. His wife had said she would be gone by evening.

You know what I was thinking by that time, don't you? *Okay, Lord. I think this is my appointment. And I accept. . . .*

"Do you want your wife to leave?" I asked. He said no.

"Open to a couple of ideas?" I offered. When he said yes, I knew it was the Lord's confirmation of another Jabez experience. I spent the next hour talking through several key biblical principles for a happy marriage. Terry hadn't heard of even one before.

By the time I was done, Terry was so anxious to give his new insights a chance to save his marriage that he jumped to his feet. "Listen, Terry," I said, "I really want to hear how things go for you and your wife today.

Whatever happens, come by the boat before we sail and tell me, okay?"

Terry agreed, waved, and was gone. By that evening, everyone was back on board. I walked the deck, waiting. I was still lonely, kind of frustrated, and starting to second-guess what had gone on inside Terry over coffee. When the captain ordered the final blast announcing our departure, I walked to the back of the ship where the crew was busy throwing off the stern lines. And there, running towards us along the shore, came a young couple hand in hand. When they got close enough to see me hanging over the rail, they started yelling. "It worked! It worked! We're together!"

The rest of the voyage I was so exhilarated at what God had done that I felt like I was floating without help from the ship. God had made an appointment for that young man and me. And He had been bringing us toward each other from the moment I had asked for a larger life in His service.

LIVING BY GOD'S MATH

Whatever our gifts, education, or vocation might be, our calling is to do God's work on earth. If you want, you can call it living out your faith for others. You can call it ministry. You can call it every Christian's day job. But whatever you call it, God is looking for people who want to do more of it, because sadly, most believers seem to shrink from living at this level of blessing and influence.

Our reluctance comes from getting our numbers right, but our arithmetic completely wrong.

For most of us, our reluctance comes from getting our numbers right, but our arithmetic completely wrong. For example, when we're deciding what size territory God has in mind for us, we keep an equation in our heart that adds up something like this:

My abilities + experience + training
+ my personality and appearance
+ my past + the expectations of others
= my assigned territory.

No matter how many sermons we've heard about God's power to work through us, we simply gloss over the meaning of that one little word *through*. Sure, we say we want God to work *through* us, but what we really mean is *by* or *in association with*. Yet God's reminder to us is the same one He gave the Jews when they returned from captivity to a decimated homeland: "Not by might nor by power but by My Spirit, says the Lord of hosts" (Zechariah 4:6).

Our God specializes in working through normal people who believe in a supernormal God who will do His work through them. What He's waiting for is the invitation. That means God's math would look more like this:

My willingness and weakness
+ God's will and supernatural power
= my expanding territory.

When you start asking in earnest—begging—for more influence and responsibility with which to honor Him, God will bring opportunities and people into your path. You can trust Him that He will never send someone to you whom you cannot help by His leading and strength. You'll nearly always feel fear when you begin to take new territory for Him, but you'll also experience the tremendous thrill of God carrying you along as you're doing it. You'll be like John and Peter, who were given the words to say at the moment they needed them.

One day in answer to Darlene's prayers for an enlarged ministry, a neighbor we hardly knew came knocking at our door. "Ma'am," she said through tears, "My husband is dying, and I have nobody to talk to. Can you help me?"

He will never send someone to you whom you cannot help.

Larger borders. An appointment to keep.

Recently on a cross-country train trip, I prayed again that God would enlarge my borders. While I was eating in the dining car, I asked the Lord to send someone who needed Him. A woman sat down across the table from me and said she needed to ask me a question. She knew my name, but little else about me. She looked deeply agitated.

"What can I do for you?" I asked.

"I'm afraid of the Antichrist," she replied. "For fifty years, I've lived in dread that I won't recognize him when he comes and that I'll be deceived by him and receive the mark of the beast."

That point-blank question from a woman

I'll never meet again led to a moving conversation and a beautiful spiritual deliverance.
Larger borders. An appointment to keep.

YOUR FRONT-ROW SEAT

To pray for larger borders is to ask for a miracle—it's that simple. A miracle is an intervention by God to make something happen that wouldn't normally happen. That, and nothing less, was what Jabez had to have to transcend his name and transform his circumstances.

Do you believe miracles still happen? Many Christians I've met do not. I remind them that miracles don't have to break natural law to be a supernatural event. When Christ stilled the storm, He didn't set aside universal law—the storm would eventually have subsided on its own. Instead, He directed the weather pattern. When Elijah prayed for it to stop raining, God directed the natural cycle of drought and rain.

In the same way, God's miracle-working powers were clearly in evidence when, knowing Terry's need, He brought us together on Patmos. And when, knowing the needs of the woman on the train, He arranged a conversation between us.

The most exhilarating miracles in my life have always started with a bold request to expand God's kingdom *a lot.* When you take little steps, you don't need God. It's when you thrust yourself in the mainstream of God's plans for this world—which are beyond our ability to accomplish—and plead with Him, *Lord, use me—give me more ministry for You!*—that you release miracles. At that moment, heaven sends angels, resources, strength, and the people you need. I've seen it happen hundreds of times.

God always intervenes when you put His agenda before yours and go for it! Amazingly, if you have prayed to the Lord to expand a border, you *will* recognize His divine answer. You'll have a front-row seat in a life of miracles.

4

The Touch
of Greatness

Oh, that Your hand would be with me!

Now you've done it. Gone over the edge. Gotten in too deep. Come up smack against the cold stone of reality. You are unable to hold on to the life you reached for. . . .

Having dared to ask for an enlarged ministry, more than a few Christians have faltered at this point in their spiritual transformation. They've received blessings on a scale they hadn't imagined possible. They've seen God stretch the limits of their influence and opportunities.

But suddenly the rush of wind under their wings stops. Helpless, they start to plummet.

Sound familiar? Maybe your new business opportunities threaten to outrun your experience and resources. Maybe the teenagers who have started congregating in your kitchen suddenly seem to be influencing your family more negatively than you are influencing them positively. Maybe the new ministry opportunities you prayed for and received are turning out to require a person with much more ability than you will ever have.

You have taken up an armload of God's blessings, marched into new territory . . . and stumbled into overwhelming circumstances. When believers find themselves in this kind of unexpected quandary, they often feel afraid. Misled. Abandoned. A little angry.

I did. . . .

DESCENDING TO POWER

Talk about plummeting! I felt out of control and weak—nothing like a leader is supposed to feel—and most days all I could see was the ground rushing up at me. It was early in my ministry adventure, after doors had started to burst open on exciting new possibilities at Walk Thru the Bible. But I just couldn't shake the feeling that I was the wrong man for the job.

Extremely upset, I decided to seek the counsel of a trusted older man. John Mitchell was in his eighties then—a Yorkshire-born Bible teacher who had been a spiritual father to thousands. I told him what I thought God was calling me to do and then confessed my problem. I was still trying to describe my crisis in some detail when he broke in.

"Son," he said, in his kindly brogue, "that feeling you are running from is called dependence. It means you're walking with the Lord Jesus." He paused to let me take in his words, then continued. "Actually, the second you're not feeling dependent is the second you've backed away from truly living by faith."

I just couldn't shake the feeling that I was the wrong man for the job.

I didn't like what I heard. "You're saying, Dr. Mitchell, that feeling that I just can't do it is what I'm *supposed* to be feeling?"

"Why certainly, young man!" he said, beaming. "That's the one all right."

It's a frightening and utterly exhilarating truth, isn't it? As God's chosen, blessed sons and daughters, we are expected to attempt something large enough that failure is guaranteed . . . unless God steps in. Take a minute to prayerfully try to comprehend how contrary that truth is to everything you would humanly choose:

- It goes against common sense.
- It contradicts your previous life experience.
- It seems to disregard your feelings, training, and need for security.
- It sets you up to look like a fool and a loser.

Yet it is God's plan for His most-honored servants.

I'll admit, big-screen heroes don't seem to put any stock in dependence—but you and I were made for it. Dependence upon God makes heroes of ordinary people like Jabez and you and me. How? We're forced to cry out with Jabez's third desperate plea:

"Oh, that Your hand would be with me!"

With that, we release God's power to accomplish His will and bring Him glory through all those seeming impossibilities.

Notice that Jabez did not begin his prayer by asking for God's hand to be with him. At that point, he didn't sense the need. Things were still manageable. His risks, and the fears that go with them, were minimal. But when his boundaries got moved out, and the kingdom-sized tasks of God's agenda started coming at him, Jabez knew he needed a divine hand—and fast. He could have turned back, or he could have tried to keep going in his own strength. Instead, he prayed.

You could call God's hand on you "the touch of greatness." You do not become great; He becomes great through you.

If seeking God's blessings is our ultimate act of worship, and asking to do more for Him is our utmost ambition, then asking for God's hand upon us is our strategic choice to sustain and continue the great things that God has begun in our lives.

That's why you could call God's hand on you "the touch of greatness." You do not become great; you become dependent on the strong hand of God. Your surrendered need turns into His unlimited opportunity. And He becomes great through you.

A LADDER TO THE CLOUDS

One day when our kids were preschoolers, Darlene and I found ourselves with them at a large city park in southern California. It was the kind of park that makes a grown man wish he were a kid again. It had swings, monkey bars, and seesaws, but what was most enticing were the slides—not just one slide, but three—from small, to medium, to enormous. David, who was five at the time, took off like a shot for the small slide.

"Why don't you go down with him?" Darlene suggested.

But I had another idea. "Let's wait and see what happens," I said. So we relaxed on a nearby bench and watched. David clambered happily to the top of the smallest slide. He waved over at us with a big smile, then whizzed down.

He peered up the ladder. In his young imagination, it must have reached to the clouds.

Without hesitation he moved over to the medium-sized slide. He had climbed halfway up the ladder when he turned and looked at me. I looked away. He pondered his options for a moment, then carefully backed down one step at a time.

"Honey, you ought to go help him out," my wife said.

"Not yet," I replied, hoping the twinkle in

my eye would reassure her that I wasn't just being careless.

David spent a few minutes at the bottom of the middle slide watching other kids climb up, whiz down, and run around to do it again. Finally his little mind was made up. He could do it. He climbed up . . . and slid down. Three times, in fact, without even looking at us.

Then we watched him turn and head toward the highest slide. Now Darlene was getting anxious. "Bruce, I don't think he should do that by himself. Do you?"

"No," I replied as calmly as possible. "But I don't think he will. Let's see what he does."

When David reached the bottom of the giant slide, he turned and called out, "Daddy!" But I glanced away again, pretending I couldn't hear him.

He peered up the ladder. In his young imagination, it must have reached to the clouds. He watched a teenage boy go hurtling down the slide. Then, against all odds, he decided to try. Step-by-step, hand over hand, he inched up the ladder. He hadn't reached a third of the way when he froze. By this time, the teenager was coming up behind him and yelled at him to get going. But David couldn't. He couldn't go up or down. He had reached the point of certain failure.

I rushed over. "Are you okay, son?" I asked from the bottom of the ladder.

He looked down at me, shaken but clinging to that ladder with steely determination. And I could tell he had a question ready.

"Dad, will you come down the slide with me?" he asked. The teenager was losing patience, but I wasn't about to let the moment go.

"Why, son?" I asked, peering up into his little face.

"I can't do it without you, Dad," he said, trembling. "It's too big for me!"

I stretched as high as I could to reach him and lifted him into my arms. Then we climbed that long ladder up to the clouds together. At the top, I put my son between my legs and wrapped my arms around him. Then we went zipping down the slide together, laughing all the way.

His Hand, His Spirit

That is what your Father's hand is like. You tell Him, "Father, please do this in me because I can't do it alone! It's too big for me!" And you step out in faith to do and say things that could only come from His hand. Afterwards, your spirit is shouting, *God did that, nobody else! God carried me, gave me the words, gave me the power—and it is wonderful!*

I couldn't recommend more highly living in this supernatural dimension!

God's power under us, in us, surging through us is exactly what turns depen-dence into unforgettable experiences of completeness. "Not that we are sufficient of ourselves," wrote Paul, "to think of anything as being from ourselves, but our sufficiency is from God, who also made us sufficient as ministers of the new covenant" (2 Corinthi-ans 3:5–6).

Tragic as it might sound, the hand of the Lord is so seldom experienced by even ma-ture Christians that they don't miss it and don't ask for it. They hardly know it exists. They think of it as something reserved for prophets and apostles, but not for them. As you'd expect, when these believers arrive at points of certain failure, they tend to come to the wrong conclusion: *I've gone too far; I've ended up in the wrong place. And since*

I already have all the resources I'm going to get, I need to exit fast!

Jabez, by contrast, was so certain that God's hand upon him was necessary for blessing that he couldn't imagine a life of honor without it. Let's look more closely at the meaning of his prayer.

The "hand of the Lord" is a biblical term for God's power and presence in the lives of His people (see Joshua 4:24 and Isaiah 59:1). In Acts, the phenomenal success of the early church was attributed to one thing: "The hand of the Lord was with them, and a great number believed and turned to the Lord" (Acts 11:21). A more specific New Testament description for God's hand is "the filling of the Holy Spirit." The church's growth bears powerful witness to both the necessity and availability of the hand of God to accomplish the business of God.

Consider the natural progression from more blessing to more territory to the need for supernatural power. When Jesus gave His disciples the Great Commission—"Go therefore and make disciples of all the nations . . . and lo, I am with you always" (Matthew 28:19–20)—He was bestowing on them both an incredible blessing and an impossible task. Into *all* the world and preach? Certainly a disaster in the making! After all, He was commissioning such unreliable cowards as Peter, who had already proved that a girl by a campfire could get him to deny he'd ever heard of Jesus!

Yet when He sent the Holy Spirit (Acts 1:8), Jesus touched these ordinary believers with greatness, filling them with His miraculous power to spread the Gospel. In fact, you'll notice in Luke's account that the phrase "filled with the Spirit" is often linked to a consequence: They "spoke with boldness" (see Acts 4:13; 5:29; 7:51; 9:27). Only God at work *through them* could account for the miracles and mass conversions that followed.

When we ask for God's mighty presence like Jabez and the early church did, we will also see tremendous results that can be explained only as from the hand of God.

What strikes me about the early church was that believers continually sought to be filled by God (see Acts 4:23–31). They were known as a community who spent hours and even days in prayer together, waiting upon God and asking for His power (see Acts 2:42–47). They were longing to receive more of God's "hand"—a fresh spiritual in-filling of

God's power that would turn impending, certain failure into a miracle and make their extraordinary assignment possible.

Paul told the Christians at Ephesus to make it a priority to be "filled with all the fullness of God" (Ephesians 3:19). To that end, he prayed that God would bless and strengthen them "with might through His Spirit" (3:16).

When was the last time your church got together and pleaded for the filling of the Spirit? When was the last time you petitioned God regularly and fervently, "Oh, put Your hand upon me! Fill me with Your Spirit!"? The rapid spread of the Good News in the Roman world couldn't have happened any other way.

TWELVE TEENS AND A DISAPPEARING EGG

Many years ago, while I was serving as a youth pastor at a large church in New Jersey, twelve high school kids proved to me that the hand of God is available to every believer who asks. For a summer ministry project we had prayerfully set our sights on suburban Long Island, New York. Objective: to evangelize the youth of the area in six weeks.

We decided on a three-part strategy. We would begin with backyard Bible studies, switch to beach evangelism in the afternoon, and then wrap it up with an evening outreach through local churches.

Parents kept telling us that what we were attempting was impossible.

Sounds simple, but I don't have to tell you that the team—youth pastor included—felt overwhelmed by the size of the task.

We invited a specialist in children's ministry on Long Island to give us some training. He told our missionary band that getting thirteen or fourteen kids in a backyard club would be a smashing success. After he left, I quietly said, "If we don't have one hundred kids in each club by the end of the week, we should consider it a failure."

Suddenly, all of us wanted to get down on our knees and pray.

I'll never forget those young, earnest prayers. "Lord, please bless us!" and "Lord, I know it's way over my head, but please, give me a hundred kids!" and "Lord, by Your Spirit, pull off something great for Your glory!"

Parents kept telling our team that what we

were attempting was impossible. And I'm sure they were right. But it started happening. Four of the six teams had more than a hundred children crammed into their meetings that first week. Some groups had to move to homes where two backyards adjoined without fences so all the kids could fit. By week's end we had shared the Good News with more than five hundred children, most of whom had never been to church.

If that wasn't enough miracles, the beach phase of our mission to Long Island brought more—helped along by a little magic. Actually, I went into a local novelty shop and came back to the group with a beginner's magic kit. You know, "everything you need to amaze and impress your friends." I stayed up until 3:00 A.M. learning how to make an egg "disappear." By the next afternoon, we were unrolling our free magic show in the sand and pleading with God for His hand to be upon us.

Specifically, we were asking the Lord for thirty decisions for salvation *by the end of the first day.*

Our audience grew from a single row of squirming children (dropped off by parents who wanted a few minutes of peace) to more than 150 bathing-suited customers. We rotated the entertainment from magic shows to storytelling to Gospel presentations. Parents began edging closer. Finally clusters of teenagers started swelling our crowd. By the end of the afternoon we had reached a count of 250. And when we finally gave an invitation, no fewer than thirty people indicated they wanted to accept Jesus Christ as their Savior—right there on the beach.

Once we had established our beach ministry, we added evening crusades for youth in local churches. God blessed our efforts beyond anyone's expectation—but right in line with the scope of our Jabez prayer. By the end of our six-week invasion, we could count twelve hundred new believers on Long Island, all of whom received helps and follow-up material.

Those twelve high school kids returned to their comfortable, middle-class lives in the suburbs convinced that *God can do anything*. The first thing that changed was their home church because they decided to pray for the Holy Spirit to move in their own congregation and bring repentance and revival.

Impossible? Not at all. Twelve kids and a

youth sponsor watched as God's hand moved through the church. As the members of the mission team shared their stories and challenged the church to ask God for more, revival swept through that church like no one could remember.

All because twelve students asked for blessings indeed, for more territory for God's glory, and for His hand of power to be upon them.

A FATHER'S TOUCH

Like any loving dad at the playground, God is watching and waiting for you to ask for the supernatural power He offers. "For the eyes of the LORD run to and fro throughout the whole earth, to show Himself strong on behalf of those whose heart is loyal to Him" (2 Chronicles 16:9). Notice that our God is not scanning the horizon for spiritual giants or seminary standouts. He eagerly seeks those who are sincerely loyal to Him. Your loyal heart is the only part of His expansion plan that He will not provide.

God is watching and waiting for you to ask.

You and I are always only one plea away from inexplicable, Spirit-enabled exploits. By His touch you can experience supernatural enthusiasm, boldness, and power. It's up to you.

Ask every day for the Father's touch.

Because for the Christian, dependence is just another word for power.